In Care

In Care

Kenneth T. Williams

In Care
first published 2017 by
Scirocco Drama
An imprint of J. Gordon Shillingford Publishing Inc.
© 2017 Kenneth T. Williams

Scirocco Drama Editor: Glenda MacFarlane
Cover design by Terry Gallagher/Doowah Design Inc.
Author Photo by Stefen Winchester

Printed and bound in Canada on 100% post-consumer recycled paper.

We acknowledge the financial support of the Manitoba Arts Council and
The Canada Council for the Arts for our publishing program.

For production info contact the author's agent,
Charles Northcote at charlesnorthcote@rogers.com or at (416) 466-4929,
or the author at kennethwilliams@shaw.ca.

Library and Archives Canada Cataloguing in Publication

Williams, Kenneth T., 1965-, author
   In care / Kenneth T. Williams. -- 1st edition.

A play.
ISBN 978-1-927922-30-9 (softcover)

   I. Title.

PS8645.I4525I5 2017   C812'.6   C2017-901071-9

J. Gordon Shillingford Publishing
P.O. Box 86, RPO Corydon Avenue, Winnipeg, MB Canada R3M 3S3

For Janice and Purple Butterfly.

Kenneth T. Williams

Kenneth T. Williams is a Cree playwright from the George Gordon First Nation in the Treaty 4 territory, and is the first Indigenous person to earn an MFA in playwriting from the University of Alberta.

His plays *Café Daughter*, *Gordon Winter*, *Thunderstick*, *Bannock Republic*, *suicide notes* and *Three Little Birds* have been produced across Canada.

In Care is his fifth play to be published by Scirocco Drama.

He is a member of the Saskatchewan Playwrights Centre, the Playwrights Guild of Canada, and the Literary Managers and Dramaturgs of the Americas. He recently served on the Indigenous Advisory Council for the National Arts Centre in Ottawa and as the interim artistic director of the Gordon Tootoosis Nīkānīwin Theatre in Saskatoon. He is returning to Edmonton after a twenty year absence to be an assistant professor at the University of Alberta's Drama Department. He and his partner, Melissa, are the loving guardians of their fourth hamster, The Grand Duchess Cinnamon Sugar Toast.

Acknowledgements

I am grateful for the financial support of the Canada Council for the Arts and the Saskatchewan Arts Board. Special thanks to Native Earth Performing Arts, Persephone Theatre's playwrights unit, the Saskatchewan Playwrights Centre, and the Gordon Tootoosis Nīkānīwin Theatre. Thank you, Yvette, for your guidance and patience. A shout out to all of the actors and dramaturges who gave their voices and talents in helping me shape this script:

Yvette Nolan, Philip Adams, Brian Quirt, Ali Joy Richardson, John Lazarus, Rachel Cantin, Samantha Brown, Kristopher Bowman, Lisa Nasson, Dawn Bird, Caitlin Vancoughnett, Mark Dieter, Jamie Lee Shebelski, Jessica Fleming, Keith Barker, Michaela Washburn, and Nicole Joy Fraser.

Production History

In Care had its world premiere at the Gordon Tootoosis Nīkānīwin Theatre, in Saskatoon, Saskatchewan on October 20, 2016.

CAST

Janice Fisher..........................Krystle Pederson

Bayley van Rijn.....................Emma Laishram

Holland Trent.................Michaela Washburn

Angel Carriere....................Aren Okemaysim

Directed by Yvette Nolan

Stage Manager: Aaron Shingoose

Production Manager: Jim Arthur

Set Design: Logan Taylor

Lighting Design: Jim Arthur

Costume Design: Jeff Chief

Sound Design: tBone

Bayley (Emma Laishram) and Holland (Michaela Washburn)
in the 2016 production of *In Care*.

Holland (Michaela Washburn) and
Angel (Aren Okemaysim)
in the 2016 production of *In Care*.

Janice (Krystle Pederson) and Bayley (Emma Laishram)
in the 2016 production of *In Care*.

Janice (Krystle Pederson) in the 2016 production
of *In Care*.

Janice (Krystle Pederson) and Angel (Aren Okemaysim)
in the 2016 production of *In Care*.

Angel (Aren Okemaysim) in
the 2016 production of *In Care*.

Foreword

Kenneth T. Williams' *In Care* is the kind of play that makes people uncomfortable, exposing difficult truths about the welfare of children in our society. Even the title is foreboding, implying that a child is not being cared for carefully enough and therefore needs to be seized by the authorities.

In Care is a tough play, following one mother on her journey to try to reclaim her children. In the process, the play exposes a system that is almost impossible to escape once you are in it.

All of the characters in the play are doing their best under the circumstances, but the system that is built to protect children is just so flawed that no matter what actions they take, someone is hurt. There is no happy ending for anyone. If there is a journey for the characters, it is one of coming to understand how the system itself is inexorable, unrelenting, and intransigent.

Everyone in our rehearsal hall had some personal connection to children who were or had been in care. Each of us told stories about foster brothers and sisters, temporary siblings, mothers we knew who had lost children, children we knew who had narrowly avoided being seized. Ken told the story of the mother who had inspired the play, a story he had not been able to tell as a journalist.

I knew when GTNT decided to produce the play that we would need to create a safe space to tell this story, not just for the actors, but for the audiences who would come to see the show. We could not in good faith lead them through Janice's story and then spit them out on the street to deal with their own feelings. Like those of us in the room, they would have known children in care, mothers who lost children. They may once have been those children; they may be those children's grandparents now.

So we decided to create a second act. Ken's play, Janice's journey in trying to get her children out of care, is a tightly wound fifty minutes or so. After an intermission, during which we offered bannock and tea, the audience came back into the theatre and a facilitator led a discussion. Each night, several invited guests spoke to begin the discussion. Social workers, lawyers, the chief of police, advocates, elders, were all members of the panels on various nights. Audience members, too, spoke about their reaction to the play; some told of experiences similar to Janice's.

The second act varied from night to night, depending on who was in the room. Surprisingly, almost all audience members stayed, choosing to return to the circle and listen. Some spoke, many did not. The only rule of the second act was that it could not be longer than the first. People in the circle who had witnessed the helplessness of Janice were given the opportunity to offer suggestions, share experiences that perhaps differed from hers, articulate possible ways forward. Some people had been surprised to learn about the challenges built into the system, and found in themselves a burgeoning empathy. Here was the possibility of change, the offer of hope, people sitting together in a circle, listening to each other, hearing each other. The dialogue that Ken begins with the play continues into the second act, out onto the street and, we hope, into everyone's daily lives.

Yvette Nolan
January 2017

Production Notes

There are no scene breaks or blackouts, the characters are on stage for the whole play. The set is minimal, suggestive, nothing that requires a lot of moving or re-setting. If anything is fixed, it must be functional and appropriate for all scenes.

The staging should be circular and unconventional. There should be plenty of room for the actors to move amongst the audience.

The numbers after the character names are based on which scene they're in. For example, BAYLEY-1 and ANGEL-1 are in Scene 1, which takes place during Angel's therapy session. The characters' names will identify the scene and who they're talking to.

The scenes are:

Scene 1   Bayley and Angel during Angel's various therapy sessions.

Scene 2   Bayley and Janice in Bayley's office at Circle Fire during various case meetings.

Scene 3   Bayley and Holland in Holland's office at Circle Fire.

Scene 4   Later with Bayley and Holland in Holland's office at Circle Fire.

Scene 5   Aboriginal awareness seminar for the police service.

Scene 6   At Dakota's graveside.

Scene 7   At Janice's apartment.

Scene 8   Bayley and Janice at a remote mine site.

Scene 9   At Circle Fire's Offices.

Scene 10 Janice's protest in front of Circle Fire's office.

Scene 11   Angel at Dakota's graveside.

Producers are encouraged to stage a "second act" that involves a discussion or other types of community engagement with the audience. This should be led by an experienced facilitator, familiar with the issues of Indigenous peoples and child welfare.

In Care

Characters

Janice Fisher.....identifies female, First Nations. Late 20s,
her children are "in care." Mother of Dakota.
Modestly dressed, clothes are functional, mismatched.

Bayley van Rijn.....identifies female, Indian/Dutch. Early 30s,
social worker and grief therapist. Her parents are from South
Africa. Clothes express her professionalism and confidence.

Holland Trent.....identifies female, First Nations. Mid 40s,
executive director of Circle Fire Family Services. Dresses in
jeans and blazer, maybe cowboy boots, never a tie, but always
with some attention-getting Indigenous-inspired jewelry
(i.e. American southwest turquoise or Plains bone choker).

Angel Carriere.....identifies male, Métis. 20s, police officer,
three years on the job. Shot and killed Dakota.
Wears police work dress uniform, but no body armour.

Scene

A major city, by Canadian standards.

Time

Now-ish.

Act I

We hear police chatter over a radio.

A gunshot.

ANGEL-1:   I hear it. Even now, I still hear it. The screaming. It was like. I mean. Can hate have a sound? I didn't know. I didn't know a girl could make a sound like that.

BAYLEY-1:   *(Reading from a report.)* The other girl had been stabbed five times.

ANGEL-1:   I don't remember reaching for my weapon. It was in my hands when I got to the top of the stairs. Dakota was on top of the other girl. It was Dakota who was screaming. Blood everywhere. Her arms were in the air. Ready to strike again.

I hit her on the collarbone. Near her left shoulder.

She twitched.

BAYLEY-1:   The report says she died instantly.

ANGEL-1:   She gasped when the bullet hit her.

SOUND: A gasp.

ANGEL-1:   But I still hear her screaming.

BAYLEY-1:   You saved that other girl's life.

JANICE-2:   Dakota's father? I don't know. Some rich, white guy. They were the only ones with enough money to buy sex without a condom. Could've been that guy who owns that big Ford dealership. You know the one. Has those annoying ads on TV with his daughter singing "No one beats Quality Ford!"

Maybe it was him. He was a regular. He said he liked the colour of my skin, that I was "prettier" than the other girls.

I was pretty then.

And he had money. He had everything. A beautiful daughter. And she must have had a beautiful mother. Because. He wasn't much too look at. And yet Quality Ford needed "pretty brown girls" like me from time to time.

Must be nice when your father gives you a sweet job like that, making commercials for television. I think I saw her on some TV series as well.

Dakota was born with cocaine in her system. I was only allowed to give her a name before she was taken from me. Taken into care. Dakota. It was the only Indian-sounding name I could think of. I wanted her to remember, you know. I wanted her to know, somehow. About me.

Yeah. I know. Fat lot of good that did her.

Maybe I should've called her Quality instead. Who knows what might have happened.

Was there a funeral?

BAYLEY-2: She was a ward of one of the child protection agencies. They took care of everything.

JANICE-2: Why didn't anyone tell me she had been shot? Didn't I have the right to know that?

BAYLEY-2: Her file had bounced around to so many different agencies that they lost track of you.

JANICE-2: Until you took my other three girls.

BAYLEY-2: It wasn't us, Janice. We just now got your file.

HOLLAND, with a newspaper.

HOLLAND-3: "Constable Angel Carriere. Cleared for active duty." This is our nine-eleven. This is the day everything changes for us. Right now, all the good will is on our side. *(Reads from the paper.)* "Failure of the child protection services to act in Dakota's best interest." "Is another child shooting only a matter of time?" *(Points at the papers.)* Now is the time to act. We are going to get those kids.

ANGEL-1: Do you know what the inquest said? They said. That I was to be commended. Not just for saving the other girl's life. But for how my skill and training ensured that when I did fire my weapon, I only hit Dakota.

BAYLEY-1: Anyone in your position would've done the same thing.

ANGEL-1: I've heard that a million times. Do you know what else I've heard? That Dakota had to be "put down" as if she was some kind of dangerous animal. That I did the world a favour.

HOLLAND-3:   Each of those kids has federal funding attached to them. Once those kids are in our care, that funding, every last dime, will go to us.

BAYLEY-3:   But they're already in care.

HOLLAND-3:   Not with Circle Fire.

BAYLEY-3:   You just can't take over another agency's files. Not without their permission.

HOLLAND-3:   They will give it. Or rather, the province will make them give it. Circle Fire is the only Aboriginal-run and controlled child protection agency in the province. After this travesty, they wouldn't dare deny us those kids.

JANICE-2:   You want to know the hard stuff, don't you. The rapes I've endured, especially the ones by cops. My near-death experiences. The drug use. The horror stories. You want me to. Eviscerate myself for you. It's pornographic, really.

BAYLEY-2:   My job isn't to say, hey, I know where you come from. My job isn't to be your friend. That would be dishonest. My job is to say, a healthy relationship with your kids is possible. Going to school, getting a job, and escaping a poisonous environment are possible. That's my job.

JANICE-2:   I did have a good relationship with my kids. They were healthy. The older ones were doing well in school. Next thing I know, children's services is at my door saying that there had been a fight in my apartment. Someone had pulled a knife. And for the safety of my children, they were being temporarily apprehended. There was no fight. There was no knife. They were taken from me because someone lied.

HOLLAND-3:   Those other agencies will fight us. They've gotten wealthy off our kids. Remember that.

ANGEL-1:   I want a family. One day. Something like my folks had. House. Marriage. Kids. Or. I wanted kids. But. I don't know anymore. It feels. Gone. I couldn't think of my future without a family. Without kids. I could see my life, had it planned, since I was twelve. At twelve. It was then I knew I was going to be a cop. And, even before then, I knew I was going to be a father.

But.

Do we really get to choose these things? Dakota didn't choose to be born like she was. It didn't matter what anyone wanted when we met.

BAYLEY-1:   Do you want Dakota's mother to forgive you?

ANGEL-1:   The inquest said I acted as any responsible person should have. In fact, they made it clear that any other action would have been a dereliction of my duty. You know what that means. At that moment, killing that little girl was my job.

And I did it well. If I did nothing wrong. If I acted correctly. Then forgiveness. It doesn't. How can I even consider it?

It doesn't matter who was at the top of the stairs that day. Dakota was going to die. Something bigger than us was happening then. That was the inevitable conclusion.

Predestined, almost.

HOLLAND-3:   When those other agencies were in charge, they were building chicken coops but expecting eagles. Low-income neighborhoods and housing projects? They're factories. Assembly lines.

Sure, once in a while, one of those chickens will take a good look at the life they're being groomed and bred for and say "I want to be an eagle. None of this chicken life for me." They will escape. We will herald their accomplishments. We will shout: "You, too, can be an eagle if you just grab your own bootstraps and give them a pull!"

And while we are blinded by their bright shiny eagleness, while we go on believing that the system works if you have the gumption for it, we blissfully ignore all of the other chickens getting marched into the slaughterhouse.

BAYLEY-3:   You sound just like my father when he talks about South Africa. About why he and my mother had to leave.

HOLLAND-3:   But you went back. For university.

BAYLEY-3:   My parents spoke about a country blessed by so much wealth and beauty, made ugly. Not by accident but by design. Even after apartheid fell. They refused to go back. My father still cannot speak to any of his family.

Then I saw a program offered by the University of Pretoria. Industrial Sociology and Labour Studies. Designed to help rebuild the "new and wonderful" post-apartheid South Africa. Gender studies. Labour actions. Globalization. This was my chance to see it for myself. Maybe connect with my father's family.

I wanted to make South Africa the place that my parents dreamed it could be. As if I was going to single-handedly undo generations of systemic brutality with this one degree. Oh my god. My classmates let me know just how naive I was. What was I doing there? I wasn't South African. I did not bear the scars of being labelled "coloured" or "Asian." They kept telling me how great Canada was. How good I had it. And my dad's family wanted nothing to do with me. Because of my Indian mother.

But here, in Canada, I am "coloured." I am "non-white." It was then very obvious for me what I needed to do.

ANGEL-1:   Dakota could've been one of my little cousins or nieces. The papers had photos. School photos, I think. She was really pretty. It's weird. Right. Because she was pretty, her life shouldn't have. I mean. It's like, her being pretty makes it more tragic. It shouldn't. I know.

There was one picture where she was smiling. The only one she where she looked like a happy girl in them. Her eyes shining. Full of life. Bright.

But all of the others.

Angry. At war.

JANICE-2:   I'm amazed she lived as long as she did.

BAYLEY-2:   I can tell you where she's buried.

JANICE-2:   And say goodbye? Pay my respects? I'm the one who got her hooked on cocaine before she was even born. I'm the one who condemned her to the life she lived.

BAYLEY-2:   You must not believe that. You were a prostitute at thirteen. Dakota was born two years later. Dakota's father raped you when you were a child. He raped a child.

JANICE-2:   He was a customer. If it was him. I mean. It could've been one of the others. But I doubt it.

Quality Ford was one of the nicer dates. He could be. Trusted.

Dates. I never thought about it. Why do we call our customers dates? It was never a date. I never got drinks or a meal. I was probably cheaper. That's capitalism for you.

It's weird but. When I saw Quality Ford's car, or thought I saw it, I would get excited. A little.

BAYLEY-2:   He was a rich man paying for naked sex. Were you going to say no? Of course not. You're going to let him buy and he knew that. He counted on it. He counted on you needing someplace safe for a few hours. He counted on you being addicted. He counted on knowing that you weren't the only child selling her body, so if you said "no" he could move on down the aisle and pick another. Saying yes meant life for another few hours. You were a child. You could not say no.

HOLLAND-3:   That's why I hired you. Plus you're kind of Indian. You know. Dot, not feather.

BAYLEY-3:   Pardon me?

HOLLAND-3:   Sorry. Bad Joke.

BAYLEY-3:   It's not funny, Holland.

HOLLAND-3: Look. A little humour helps now and then.

BAYLEY-3: When appropriate. We have a new file. From the other agencies, like you wanted. You should recognize the name.

HOLLAND reads the file.

HOLLAND-3: Janice Fisher? It doesn't ring.

BAYLEY-3: Dakota's mother.

HOLLAND-3: She's still in the system?

BAYLEY-3: She was out for a while. Now she's back in. The Catholic agency apprehended her three girls. A neighbour claimed that a fight broke out in her apartment. Someone pulled out a knife.

HOLLAND-3: Passed every drug test since apprehension. Upgraded her education. Good assessment from the psychologist. Oh, that was you. Her girls. Same father?

BAYLEY-3: What does that... She's a good mother and ready to get her children back. I've supervised her most recent visits. They have been very positive for her, as well as for her girls.

HOLLAND-3: Her living situation?

BAYLEY-3: More than adequate.

HOLLAND-3: Did she move out of that building? Where the fight "allegedly" happened?

BAYLEY-3: She can't afford to live anywhere else.

HOLLAND-3: Then have the neighbours moved?

BAYLEY-3:   No. They're still there. But I have trouble believing their complaint against her. They were having their own problems with social services and were trying to deflect attention to someone else. Couldn't keep their stories straight. I've looked over her file. She's a good mother.

HOLLAND-3:   Bayley. Perception is everything right now. We're being watched. Like hawks. And we need to treat Janice's file very carefully. People still remember the shooting.

BAYLEY-3:   Yes, because you made sure of that.

HOLLAND-3:   The press played it up. I just had to show them what was really going on. It was them who made the case that an agency like Circle Fire was needed. But here's the thing. You know what never makes the news? When we do our jobs right. We have the toughest job in the world. We can never make a mistake. And no one, not one person, notices the 99.9999 per cent of the time when we do it right. That never, ever makes the news. Because it means our clients are invisible, out of sight, not a concern. "The system is working" and the sheep can continue sleepwalking. We can't have anything go wrong with her file or else those same stupid sheep in the press will be all over us. I got Circle Fire because of them. They can take it away.

Trust me, no one really cares if an Indian mother can't have her babies back.

JANICE-2:   This latte you bought me costs. About as much as I spend on food for one day. For all of us. As a treat, I would take my kids to McDonald's. The one downtown. The one that's not there anymore because the owner of the building didn't like Indians sitting on the benches in front of it. It was the only treat I could give them.

Every Saturday, we'd walk there and I'd buy them an ice cream. Or, if I had a little money left over at the end of the month, a burger and some fries. Nothing with a toy though. I couldn't afford three meals, so we'd all share. You can't share a toy. I had enough to worry about. I didn't need world war three breaking out in the middle of McDonald's because I couldn't buy them all a toy. The girls don't know why we can't go there anymore. I don't know if I understand it. Because someone was sitting on a bench? Really? It means I have to find another place for our treat day.

BAYLEY-2:   Your housing situation. You have to find another place.

JANICE-2:   Another place? With my babies in care, social assistance has reduced my income. The landlord is only letting me stay because this was supposed to be "temporary." If I don't get my kids back I'll lose the only place I could ever afford for them.

BAYLEY-2:   We could find you a job.

JANICE-2:   No one will hire me. Not even to sell donuts and pour coffee.

BAYLEY-2:   There's a trainee position available at one of the mines.

JANICE-2:   The mines! Up north. Hundreds of miles away from my babies. Is that what I should do? Because I know what kind of job I'll get there. I'm very well qualified for it.

BAYLEY-2:   It could be a new beginning for you. Even a career.

ANGEL-1:   I wanted to be a police officer because I wanted to help people. How often have you heard that? How often have I said it whenever I've gone into schools to talk to kids about my job?

I've always been good at school. It wasn't hard. I liked school. And I was always athletic. I have my black belt in judo. And university. I have a degree in psychology. Thinking law in the future.

All part of the "plan," right?

HOLLAND-4:   I need your help with this proposal.

BAYLEY-4:   A safe house? We barely have the staff to keep up with the case files we have now.

HOLLAND-4:   Look, the feds and the province have agreed to co-fund safe houses for women who are fleeing abusive partners, husbands, whatever. They are not going to do this again, believe me. So we have to get on this while we can.

BAYLEY-4:   It's too early.

HOLLAND-4:   Some property is available in the west side. We can get it cheap. Wouldn't cost much to get it up to code.

BAYLEY-4:   You just can't throw a thing like this together in a few weeks. It takes planning. It takes research. How big? How long can we house the women there? Children?

HOLLAND-4:   All good questions. Which makes me think you'd be the best candidate to lead this project.

BAYLEY-4:   I can't just abandon my case files. I've established trust with these women.

HOLLAND-4:   What if I made you Deputy Director?

BAYLEY-4:   I can't. Just. Now?

HOLLAND-4:   And a pay raise. A hefty one.

BAYLEY-4:   I still want to keep some cases.

HOLLAND-4:   Only a few.

BAYLEY-4:   You let me choose whom, and you have a deal.

HOLLAND-4:   Deal.

BAYLEY-4:   Janice Fisher.

HOLLAND-4:   This new shelter is going to take a lot of your time. I could easily have one of the newer case workers take over her file.

BAYLEY-4:   I thought we would be different than the other agencies? They kept shuffling her from one case worker to the next.

HOLLAND-4:   Okay, okay. Fair enough.

BAYLEY-4:   And I want to be able to move on her file as I see fit.

ANGEL-1:   I'm going to receive a commendation from the Chief of Police.

BAYLEY-1:   Yes. I saw the story in the paper. He calls you a hero.

ANGEL-1:   Yeah, "hero." I'm also being called a murderer.

BAYLEY-1:   But you know. Right. That you're not.

ANGEL-1:   I know I did what I was trained to do.

BAYLEY-1:   Those other people weren't there.

ANGEL-1:   But they may have a point. Why didn't I. Shoot to wound? Tackle her? Use my baton? Why didn't I do anything else? Because there was nothing else, there were no other options, except what I was trained to do.

BAYLEY-1:   Can you tell me what that feels like?

ANGEL-1:   I want to know where she's buried. I'm not telling you to tell me. Or asking. I'm a cop. I can find that out myself. That's what it feels like. It makes me feel like I want to visit her. I need to see her grave.

BAYLEY-1:   What about the girl you saved? Don't you want to see her? Find out how she's doing?

HOLLAND-5:   Wow. A room full of cops. The younger me would be crapping her pants right now. *(Laughs at her joke, then.)*

               Trauma. Pain. That's what you have to remember when you, inevitably, run into the clients from Circle Fire. These women, Aboriginal women, are coping as best as they can with unbelievable trauma and pain.

But the injuries aren't visible because the damage is here. *(Points to her head.)*

And here. *(Points to her heart.)*

These injuries will not heal on their own. Not like bone. Not like skin. Your brain can't do that with psychological trauma.

How can I explain this?

Imagine. Being hit by a car. Every single day of your life. Psychologically, that's what my clients are dealing with. The brain will try to suppress the trauma. Hide it. Bury it. And if that's not enough, the person who is hurt will use anything to fight the pain, cover it up or replace it with something more manageable.

And I mean anything. Not just drugs and alcohol. I mean sex. I mean violence. Of course, you will be the first ones to deal with it, up close and in person. They will project all the pain onto you and strike out.

I'm not asking you to be superhuman. Just remember that these women, my clients at Circle Fire, are psychologically getting hit by a car. Every. Single. Day.

Polite applause.

HOLLAND-5: Thank you. Hiy-Hiy. Kinanaskomitin.

ANGEL approaches HOLLAND.

ANGEL-5: So. You're now giving Aboriginal awareness workshops to the police.

HOLLAND-5: Just trying to help. Hopefully, it sinks in.

ANGEL-5:   Yeah, those were nice words. Compassionate. It made me wonder. You know. This was the same person who threw me under the bus and made me the poster child for all that was wrong with social services and the justice system.

HOLLAND-5:   That's a bit harsh.

ANGEL-5:   You called Dakota's death a "state-sanctioned murder."

HOLLAND-5:   I called the state a murderer. Not you.

ANGEL shows HOLLAND a newspaper.

ANGEL-5:   You called me "The Angel of Death."

We see a small grave marker with just "Dakota" written on it.

ANGEL-6:   You sure this is the place? It doesn't look like a fresh grave.

BAYLEY-6:   She was cremated.

ANGEL-6:   Cremated?

BAYLEY-6:   Saves money.

ANGEL-6:   There are a lot of other markers here.

BAYLEY-6:   It's one plot.

ANGEL-6:   Like. A mass grave.

BAYLEY-6:   Anything else would be considered extravagant.

ANGEL-6:   Extravagant? Who gets to choose what "extravagant" is?

JANICE-2: The only child I'm allowed to see is buried in an unkempt corner of a city graveyard. It takes me an hour and a half to walk there from my place. I can't take the bus. Welfare took my bus pass away because I don't have my girls. And I don't want to see the other mothers on the bus. I envy their struggle to get the stroller through that tiny door and up those steps. I even envy the dirty looks the other passengers give them when they try to get that stroller down the aisle.

So I walk. I try to avoid certain roads because someone like me, walking alone, must be a hooker. I even try walking with a stroller. It doesn't matter. The men shout. When I don't respond, when I keep walking, they shout louder, thinking I can't hear them. And they laugh. And they call me names.

Horrible, dehumanizing names.

I keep walking. Most have their laugh and drive on. Once in a while though, one will go out of his way to make me stop.

SOUND: Car slowing to a stop.

JANICE-2: Pull the car in front of me. He will get out. He will try to grab me. Because ignoring him is a sin and I must pay for that sin. The man was talking and I must obey. Do I need to be reminded of this? Do I need a lesson?

And.

That's the car.

I know when I can't do this any more. When I'm done. When I'm finished. That's the car I'll get into. He won't have to take me. I will climb right in.

ANGEL-6:　　　So where are her other children?

BAYLEY-6:　　I cannot tell you that.

ANGEL-6:　　　I'm not asking. Again, it's what I'm feeling. I need to know where they are. I need to know they're okay.

BAYLEY-6:　　They're in our care.

HOLLAND-5:　I admit that was. Harsh. I'm free for a bit. Want to grab. A coffee? I can feel you need to. You know. Unpack some. You have issues about that.

ANGEL-5:　　　I don't want to grab a coffee with you. Why would you even think that? You made a lot of noise when I was cleared by the inquiry.

HOLLAND-5:　It wasn't about you. Specifically. It was about the system.

JANICE-2:　　　I'm not ready to jump into that car just yet. I will keep walking. For as long as my spirit will carry me.

> *JANICE enters the scene with BAYLEY and ANGEL at the graveside. Pause, then JANICE embraces ANGEL.*

JANICE-6:　　　Forgive me.

ANGEL-6:　　　Forgive you?

JANICE-6:　　　I didn't know it would. End here. Like it did. How could it not? I'm sorry it was you at the top of the stairs. I'm sorry I did that.

ANGEL-5:   You took advantage of me.

HOLLAND-5:   Advantage? I think that's a little. Okay. Maybe. Maybe I did. There was a greater good. What happened between you and Dakota happens a lot. We're so used to it, it's just another news item. Indian kid blah blah blah dies in care blah blah blah. It's only a matter of time before it happens again. Look. I won't apologize for what I did. It was unfortunate that you took the hit. But, really, come on. You're a hero.

ANGEL-5:   Because I chose to shoot that little girl.

HOLLAND-5:   But in the circumstances. I mean. Really.

JANICE-6:   She was never going to get better. What I did to her when she was. Inside me. When I was carrying her. She would carry that forever.

ANGEL-5:   I could have let her live.

HOLLAND-5:   Then the other girl would be dead.

ANGEL-5:   Imagine any nightmare with a child and I've seen it. Touched it. Abandoned. Neglected. The worst ones are when they don't react. When they are so far gone. When as infants they've already given up on this world.

                It's a stare. A silence. You don't forget. Can't forget. You hold them, feel their warmth, feel their breath and heartbeat and yet. There's nothing in their eyes.

                Dakota was screaming, she was alive, she was fighting something. The other little girl. She had nothing in her eyes.

JANICE-6:   Even when I was carrying her, I never felt her. Not really. I was too busy hooking and shooting up. Right now. This is the closest I've been to her. Ever. When she was born they wouldn't let me hold her.

JANICE hums to DAKOTA.

JANICE-6:   I don't know any lullabies. I would just sing along to the radio with my other girls.

BAYLEY-6:   You need to eat, Janice.

JANICE-6:   I can't. Not until my girls are back with me. The silence in my apartment. It's oppressive. Their bedroom is... I see their beds and it's like looking at empty caskets. Each day the silence rots the air. But it won't matter much longer. My landlord will evict me soon. I can't afford the place without them. And I can't bear to live there. When they're not there.

The sun is warm here. I should live here. Be next to Dakota. Her silence makes sense. Makes me warm. Feeds me.

BAYLEY-6:   Janice. You were doing really well. It's just a little longer. That's all. And it would speed up if you took the job in the mine. They'll train you. House you. Feed you. Pay you. Prove you're capable of.

JANICE-6:   I did everything you told me to do.

BAYLEY-6:   We're telling you to take the job.

JANICE-6:   I will have to live in a work camp. You judged my two-bedroom apartment unsafe, what are you going to say about a work camp? You think. After all you've put me through. I can trust your promises now?

ANGEL-6:   *(To Janice.)* Let me take you home.

JANICE-6:   Where would that be?

BAYLEY-6:   Whatever it is you're up to, Angel. This is not healthy for either of you. Especially, Janice. If she associates with you. Or. Bonds.

ANGEL-6:   If she makes a friend, that'll work against her?

BAYLEY-6:   You are not trying to be a friend, Angel. You are trying to deal with the hurt you are feeling. This is not how you should deal with it. It only delays what you need to do and it could be highly detrimental for her.

ANGEL-6:   I'm a police officer. She's a threat to herself. It would be unprofessional for me to ignore this.

BAYLEY-6:   And what are you going to do? Arrest her? Take her to the cells till she calms down. Get a judge to order seven days of mandatory supervision. All of that ends up in her file. No agency, anywhere, will give her girls back if you do that.

ANGEL-6:   Then what do we do that does not end up in her file?

BAYLEY-6:   You are taking this too personally.

ANGEL-6:   I shot her little girl! How else should I take it!

ANGEL takes JANICE home.

ANGEL-7:   I can help you, you know. I can get you certain things. Services. Groceries even.

JANICE-7:   And if that gets written down somewhere, how do you think that'll make me look? My neighbours talk. I'm sure someone is on the phone to social services to report your visit. Contact with the police is never good for people like me.

ANGEL-7:   I'm only trying.

JANICE-7:   What! Get my girls back.

ANGEL-7:   I can't. That's.

JANICE-7:   Then it would be better for all of us if you didn't interfere. I know you mean well and you think this is helping but. You are in that uniform.

ANGEL-7:   Bayley says your girls are very well taken care of.

JANICE-7:   They won't even let me see them. I'm labeled "defiant." "Oppositional." "Unbalanced" because I got angry when they took my girls. Are you allowed to be angry? Were you angry when you were called a murderer? I'm not allowed to be angry. I can't speak of my frustration. I must allow the hurt to fester unspoken. Any questions, any actions show me to be unreasonable and incapable of caring for my own children. And I did nothing! I did nothing wrong.

    SOUND: A little girl's laugh.

JANICE-7:   I miss the mornings when I'd wake up thinking I heard them giggling, or fighting, or making too much noise and. The pain. That would slowly knife its way through my chest. Because it was just a ghost of a memory. Now I wake up knowing they're not here. I would rather have the pain because I could still hear them, smell them, feel them. Their ghosts are gone and this place.

But if I leave.

ANGEL-7:   Do you want your girls to start their lives here? Or, worse, on the streets? Do you want them to learn what you had to learn when you were thirteen? I know it's not fair. I know it sucks. You must not give up on yourself. Or give up on your kids. I know the mine is far away from your girls. At least there, you know, you have a chance. It's an opportunity to make something better. You must get your kids out of care. And do everything you can to do it. Give up this place. This is not your future. Say goodbye to the ghosts. And get your actual children back.

JANICE-7:   You really believe I'll get my children back.

ANGEL-7:   I have to. (*Taps his uniform.*) Or this no longer matters. I need to believe I'm making a difference. I need to know that I'm part of a system that cares.

SOUND: a drum beat.

JANICE dons a hardhat and work gloves, and holds up a time card.

JANICE-8:   I'm fitting in, I guess. Some of the guys are crude. No different than anywhere else. I guess. This is funny. One of the other girls here kept talking about how I was some stupid squaw getting a job because my band signed a treaty with the company. Band? I don't even have a treaty card. Anyway. My boss got really mad at her. And in front of everybody he said he would fire the next person he heard speaking like that. That shut them up. He's really nice. My boss. He's gay.

BAYLEY-8:   You shouldn't. Janice. That's not.

JANICE-8:   He told me he was gay. He wanted to know about two-spirited people. I didn't know what he was talking about. I didn't grow up knowing that. He got all embarrassed. And worried. It's tough for him up here. He can't be open about it. I have it bad enough. I can only imagine what he'd have to deal with. I think he was looking for some acceptance from someone. I told him his secret was safe with me. Who am I to judge.

BAYLEY-8:   So, you're liking it up here?

JANICE-8:   When can I see my girls again?

BAYLEY-8:   There's a process, Janice. Small steps. You're getting there.

JANICE-8:   But I don't know how far "there" is. I did what you said. I'm just asking you to keep your promises after I kept mine.

BAYLEY-8:   A judge needs to have confidence that you are transitioning to a stable life.

JANICE-8:   It feels like punishment.

BAYLEY-8:   It's not punishment. It's a positive step for you. This is your first job. Right?

JANICE-8:   I'm only doing this to get them back.

BAYLEY-8:   That kind of attitude is not helpful.

JANICE-8:   What more do you want?

BAYLEY-8:   It's not about what we want.

JANICE-8:   Yes. It is. How much is enough for you people?

BAYLEY-8:   It's more than just what you do. It's about why.

JANICE-8:   I'm doing it for my girls. They are the most important people in my life. But if this is just another exercise in power for you, what difference does it make why or what I do? You're holding my children for a ransom that I can never pay.

BAYLEY-9:   You're selling the shelter's building.

HOLLAND-9:   The neigbourhood is gentrifying. Lots of people in the area were nervous about having the shelter close to their fancy new condos. So I leveraged that to buy six houses in a different area of the city. And hey, the city and the province threw in some extra cash as a goodwill gesture. We can hire more staff.

BAYLEY-9:   But the shelter.

HOLLAND-9:   Relax. We're only moving it. And making it bigger. We got the resources now.

BAYLEY-9:   For six shelters?

HOLLAND-9:   No, no, they won't all be shelters. I've got something bigger planned.

Hands BAYLEY a folder. She reads it.

BAYLEY-9:   Culturally appropriate incarceration? What.

HOLLAND-9:   Feds love this.

BAYLEY-9:   A private prison?

HOLLAND-9:   It's a state-of-the-art incarceration facility for non-violent female offenders. Aboriginal offenders.We'll have elders and cultural leaders on staff, as well as psychologists and social workers on hand. The best part is that we'll have a program that will allow the women to keep their younger children with them as part of the rehabilitation process.

BAYLEY-9:   Babies in jail?

HOLLAND-9:   It's not a jail. There will be no bars. No fences. Look, the Dutch have been running these kinds of centres for years and with amazing success.

BAYLEY-9:   With babies?

HOLLAND-9:   No, not with babies. That's our ground-breaking approach.

BAYLEY-9:   Where's the research to back that up?

HOLLAND-9:   We have plenty on how mothers do better with drug and alcohol rehabilitation if they maintain a connection with their children. The same must be true with incarceration.

BAYLEY-9:   One, we don't know that for sure. And two, it's still a jail for profit.

HOLLAND-9:   Non-profit. And once they see the success of this centre, we'll be able to start working on one for youth. Maybe men.

JANICE-8:   It's like I'm serving a sentence up here. Two weeks at a time. The camp has rules, a strict schedule. A curfew. This is no place for children, Miss Van Rijn. Forget daycare. All the things we're not supposed to have, we have plenty of. Drugs. Booze. Sex. My shift is twelve hours long. And I'm underground for most of it and exhausted when I'm done. If there's no chance for me to visit my girls, then why should I go back to the city? And they can't come up here and visit.

BAYLEY-8:   This is a chance for you to gain some independence. Use your time off to get your driver's license. Buy a car. You have the money now. Get a better place.

JANICE-8:   On my two weeks off, is that when I'm supposed to raise my kids? I don't have anyone I can leave them with. No family. Definitely no friends who I would trust with the girls. Do I keep putting them into care every time I have to do two weeks up here? And they keep asking me to take extra shifts. It doesn't look good if you keep saying no. They don't care I'm trying to get my kids back. They just want me, down in that hole, soldering wires.

             SOUND: Horn sounds the change of shift.

JANICE-8:   I have to go. When can I see my girls again?

BAYLEY-8:   I'll see about scheduling. We'll have to time it with when they're not so busy with school. When are your two weeks up?

             JANICE walks away from her.

BAYLEY-8:   Janice?

ANGEL kneels at DAKOTA's graveside.

BAYLEY-8:   Janice!

ANGEL-11:   What were you fighting? There was a fire inside you. I saw it.

BAYLEY-8:   Janice.

JANICE returns with a sign. It reads "Hunger Strike!"

HOLLAND drops some coins in front of her.

JANICE-10:   Excuse me!

HOLLAND-10:   "Hunger strike." Sorry. Thought you were asking for change.

JANICE-10:   I did everything your agency and other agencies told me to do to get my girls back. But it's not enough. It's never enough.

HOLLAND-10:   You have to move. You can't stay here, in front of the office. With that sign.

JANICE-10:   You're not giving me the options that I need.

HOLLAND-10:   Those are your only options. This, this won't work for you.

BAYLEY-9:   We should be dismantling these structures and facilities, not building new ones. How will this help us reunite children with their mothers?

HOLLAND-9:   We have to play the game for a bit.

BAYLEY-9:   We were supposed to be different, Holland. We were supposed to have values that made us better than the others.

JANICE-10:   I need my children back, Miss Trent. I will go to the media if I have to.

HOLLAND-10:   Go ahead. Try and talk to the media. See if any of them will bother. They've got terrorists and global warming and a shiny new prime minister. What are you compared to all of that?

BAYLEY-9:   We were not supposed to be "playing" games.

HOLLAND-9:   What are you accusing me of, exactly? I've been very clear about our mission here. Children. Protecting the children. Since we've taken control of the Aboriginal files, not one child has died.

ANGEL-11:   I hear you screaming. When I dream. When I'm awake. Except now. When I'm here. Now. You're silent.

BAYLEY-9:   Not one child has been returned to her mother.

HOLLAND-9:   That's not our. Bayley. When we got those files, many were incomplete. They were missing important paperwork. Like. Birth certificates. Health records. Addresses. It was the other agencies who lost track of those mothers. We cannot be held responsible for what those other agencies did before we got the files. You know this.

BAYLEY-9:   And if one of those mothers showed up at our doors looking for her child?

HOLLAND-9:   Has that happened yet? I don't see a lineup.

JANICE-10:   I'm a mother. Who did nothing wrong.

ANGEL-11:   I'm here. Say something.

HOLLAND-10: Who also walked away from a great job. That mine pays more than I make. It makes me wonder why I'm still here, slaving away, trying to make your lives better. Don't be ungrateful. Go back to the job.

BAYLEY-9: What about Janice Fisher?

HOLLAND-9: We are under a brighter microscope than any other agency. They were allowed to screw up many, many times before we came along. You think we're going to get the same leeway from the government. Or the media. We have to be extra cautious.

BAYLEY-9: It's Janice who's under the microscope. We are putting too much pressure on her. We need to let up or she'll.

HOLLAND-9: We're simply asking her to be a better. To get some life skills. To become independent. That's all.

BAYLEY-9: She was a good mom.

ANGEL-11: What are you trying to say?

HOLLAND-9: She is a prostitute. A drug addict. Her first baby was born addicted to cocaine.

BAYLEY-9: That was when she was just a kid! She was no older than Dakota when she was on the streets.

HOLLAND-9: It doesn't matter, Bayley! If we give her her children back and something goes wrong, do you think anyone will care that these things were in her past? One mistake. That's all it takes. We do not have the luxury of do-overs in child welfare. We have to be right every, single time.

Someone got it wrong with Dakota. We will never let that happen.

ANGEL-11:   I'm listening. Please. I need. I have to know.

HOLLAND-9:   Bayley, I think you're getting. It's getting personal for you, isn't it? Maybe your judgment.

BAYLEY-9:   My judgment is what, Holland?

HOLLAND-9:   You're overworked. Don't burn out on me. I can't lose you.

BAYLEY-9:   Are we guided solely by dollars?

HOLLAND-9:   If we're not, then we're in a lot of trouble. If we mismanage our funding, you can guarantee every screeching hound out there will be howling about Indians not being able to handle money or responsibility.

BAYLEY-9:   Money and public opinion.

HOLLAND-9:   Never underestimate public opinion.

JANICE-10:   You don't want the attention.

ANGEL-11:   I can barely hear you.

HOLLAND-10: I don't know if you've read a paper lately, but we are getting a lot of attention. Good attention. Great attention. The province just audited us. We run cleaner, meaner and leaner than any other child welfare agency. In fact, my agency is so good, my employees are getting poached by the government and other agencies in other provinces. We are the model now. Aboriginal kids in Aboriginal care.

BAYLEY-9:   There it is again. Can you hear it? Even when you talk to me like this, there's still "hope" in your voice. The hope you want me, you want Janice to cling to, that something better is coming. There's this bright shining light over the horizon that you say is a better world. We must keep faith with you. That the sacrifices we make are worth it for that distant light.

That light isn't coming closer. It's an illusion. We focus on it to delude ourselves that it exists.

JANICE-10:   I am not real to you? Is that it? The way I speak, the clothes I wear make you ignore me. Make you question everything I say. As if those things determine if I'm really able to feel. To think. To make the best decisions possible. Determine if I'm doing the best I can for my girls.

You.

You are allowed to do that to me. You are allowed to call me unreasonable. Unfit.

Because I fight it. I have to fight it. I am real. I am alive.

For now.

SOUND: A car slowing down. The horn beeps.

JANICE considers the car.

JANICE-10:   But I can only take so much.

SOUND: *A scream of something alive, a soul trapped in hell, screaming to get out, screaming for life, screaming because it is the only thing left to say.*

SOUND: *A shot. A gasp.*

JANICE hums a little. A little girl laughs.

The End.